MASTERPIECES IN MINIATURE
DOLLHOUSES

BOOK ONE:
MINIATURE DOLLS

NICK FORDER

APPLE

A QUARTO BOOK

Published by Apple Press
6 Blundell Street
London N7 9BH

ISBN: 1-84092-199-4

QUAR.MDC

This book was conceived, designed and produced by:
Quarto Publishing plc
The Old Brewery 6 Blundell Street
London N7 9BH

Project Editors: Nicola Birtwisle, Joyce Bentley
Senior Art Editor: Penny Cobb
Copy Editor: Sarah Vickery
Designer: Ruth Shane
Photographer: Nick Forder

Art Director: Moira Clinch
Publisher: Piers Spence

Manufactured in Hong Kong by Regent Publishing Services Ltd.
Printed in China by Leefung-Asco Printers Ltd.
9 8 7 6 5 4 3 2 1

CONTENTS

INTRODUCTION

Today's collectors of dollhouse miniatures hold differing views on whether to include dolls in a house or room setting. Often it is felt that badly posed dolls are the only aspect of miniature interiors that do not appear realistic. But on the other hand, figures engaged in action within a setting can help to tell the viewer a story, as well as establish the period of the house.

Whereas wooden furniture can be created with wood, silverware can be fashioned from silver, and ceramics are made from ceramic, it will always be impossible to make figures from actual substance. However, the advent of modern materials has enabled dollhouse dolls to evolve from poorly scaled playthings into detailed miniature people full of personality and life. Working in 1:12 scale, doll artists now create figures with

FAR LEFT: *Figure of Agnès Sorel, La Dame de Beauté, by Cassandra Hipwell.*

LEFT: *Handsome Tudor figure created by artist Jill Bennett.*

ABOVE: *Late Elizabethan merchant couple, c.1580, also by Jill Bennett.*

LEFT: *Late nineteenth-century German toymaker made by Gudrun Kolenda.*

unmistakable characters of their own, dressed in accurate costumes, with expressive facial features.

When choosing a figure, a number of different factors should be considered. Is it dressed in the period of its intended setting? Will it stand or sit appropriately? Does it have the right expression? Is its quality consistent with its posed pieces? And, most important, is this the doll you really desire?

This book contains examples made by the best doll artists

working today. Although different materials and techniques have been used in the construction and finishing of each doll, in each case, the result is superb. The dolls selected for inclusion here ultimately represent a personal choice.

Dollhouse and miniature collecting, and the method in which these tiny marvels are put together, is an individual and personal pleasure. It is intended that this book, within the series, will give the reader an insight into the wonderful world of miniatures.

Above left: *Victorians on safari, also by Gudrun Kolenda.*

Above right: *Mother Goose, created by Marcia Backstrom.*

TUDORS *and* ELIZABETHANS

KINGS AND QUEENS, LORDS AND LADIES, AND OTHER LESS REGAL PEOPLE HAVE ALL BEEN DEPICTED IN EXQUISITE DETAIL BY DOLL ARTISTS. HERE ARE SOME OF THE FINEST.

A Lady of the Court

HEIGHT: 5 ½ in (140 mm)

Riding side-saddle in her finery, this fair Tudor maiden is clearly of noble birth. Her dress is made of silk, with full sleeves lined with gold brocade of a contrasting color. The second color is also used for the underskirt and cape. Gold trims the ensemble, while tiny fleur-de-lys, also in gold, have been hand-painted onto the fabric. She wears rings on her fingers, pointed shoes of fine leather, and pendants of stones on a gold chain around her neck. The doll has been made and dressed by Louise Goldsborough of Angelique Miniatures. The horse was made by Annie Willis of Fine Design and is covered with fur. It has a saddle and bridle of real leather and a head shield of solid silver.

Tudor Market People

Average height: 6 in (153 mm)

The exact occupation or daily life of this couple is a little uncertain because the style of clothes they are wearing was very commonplace in the last part of the 16th century. Nevertheless, it might be supposed that she is a farmer's wife who has walked to the market in the nearest town to sell her seasonal produce. He is a working man, perhaps trading in the town or accompanying his wife. Both have been made by Jill Bennett and have arms and legs that can be fully posed wired to metal bodies. Their heads are made of porcelain and have hand-painted details. Their clothes are made from an assortment of fine cotton or wool fabrics, which have been "aged" to show that these are working people.

Two Liverymen c.1460

AVERAGE HEIGHT: 6 in (153 mm)

Liverymen were the heads of the medieval merchant guilds and, therefore, rich and prosperous. Naturally they dressed according to their wealth and station. Here the older man wears a slightly old-fashioned tunic, as might befit his years. His hat, or "liripipe," evolved from a single snood of an earlier time, which has been elongated and reshaped. The younger liveryman wears a more modern, belted, slightly shorter tunic and classic "liripipe." The wearing of a short tunic was the privilege of the aristocracy. Both figures were made as a special commission by Jill Bennett, with porcelain heads and self-standing metal bodies that can be posed.

A Group of Tudor Servants

AVERAGE HEIGHT: 5 ½ in (140 mm)

The costumes of these kitchen servants are made of the plainest cotton fabrics. The dolls are the creation of artist Jill Bennett, who, together with fellow artist James Carrington, perfected the unique design of constructing miniature figures with porcelain heads and self-standing, metal bodies that can be fully posed.

Tudor Family

HEIGHT: 6 in (153mm)

This family represents English merchant class status. Their clothes are well tailored and made from fine fabrics such as silk and hand-worked lace. Note the details of the little girl's apron and the britches of the father and the son. Not visible in the picture is the pomander (scented bag) that hangs from the lady's waist. Their one-of-a-kind heads are made from porcelain by artist Jill Bennett.

17th-Century Vegetable Seller

HEIGHT: 6 in (153 mm)

American artists Janet Middlebrook and Marcia Backstrom collaborated to create this French street trader. The figure was first modeled, and then recast in plastic resin, before finally being hand-painted. The costume is made from fine velvet trimmed with lace braids. The stylish wig was also specially made for this doll.

Queen Elizabeth and Robert Dudley

AVERAGE HEIGHT: 5 ¾ in (146 mm)

This figure of Queen Elizabeth I shows her as a young queen; she stands with Robert Dudley, Earl of Leicester. Both are made from Sylvia Mobley's doll kits, and dressed by miniaturist Cookie Ziemba. Queen Elizabeth has pearl earrings attached to her wig, a historically correct detail, while her sleeves and ruff are made from antique lace.

Queen Elizabeth I

HEIGHT: 5 ½ in (140 mm)

There is no mistaking this regal figure so beautifully dressed in typical period attire of gold brocade decorated with extra gold threads. The cuffs are finished with lace. Jewels in the form of a tiara, earrings, and rows of long necklaces have been added to great effect. The doll was made from a modern modeling medium by specialist doll artist James Carrington, who subsequently wigged and dressed it. The face of each doll that Carrington produces is individually modeled in order to create an expression that is just right. His experience in both costume and theater gives each one of his miniature figures a superb quality of presence. Note the very high hairline and unsmiling face of this figure, so characteristic of Queen Elizabeth I.

John Hall

Height: 6 in (153 mm)

This figure by Jill Bennett was based on the son-in-law of William Shakespeare, John Hall. Hall was, in fact, a herbalist, and although he is dressed here as a gentleman, this attire might be for everyday use, and would not be his "Sunday best." Nevertheless his costume is true of late Elizabethan style. He has a metal body construction, with fully bendable arms and legs. This allows the doll to stand or sit, or be positioned in any number of poses. The doll's head is of hand-painted porcelain with added hair and beard styled in keeping with both the times and his position. The figure stands beside an all-wood armchair with a carved back. This piece was made by miniature furniture maker David Hurley.

1649

The AGE *of* ELEGANCE

THE GEORGIAN AND REGENCY PERIODS WERE A TIME OF REFINEMENT AND BEAUTY, SHOWN HERE IN THE FINELY CRAFTED CREATIONS OF THE BEST ARTISTS.

High-Fashion Georgian

HEIGHT: 5 ½ in (140 mm)

This fully poseable doll, made by the artist James Carrington, has finely chiseled features modeled in polymer clay. She wears an elaborate yellow court dress, made from silk and trimmed with lace, with panniers—hoops—in the skirt to hold it out and make it fuller. This dress style is a little ahead of its time as court fashions always preceded popular taste. Her hat is in the exaggerated style of the period, being rather oversized and trimmed with all types of decorations, including ribbons, more lace, and a huge feather. Almost a caricature, the lady carries not only a beautifully wrapped gift, perhaps a birthday present, but also a most superior, haughty air.

Sally Fairfax

HEIGHT: 5½ in (140 mm)

Through highly detailed research into her subject, Cookie Ziemba is able to recreate characters incorporating the highest detail. Here her figure of Sally Fairfax is dressed in the style of the late 18th century. She has an undershirt made from antique lace and an overdress made of pale blue silk finished with gold colored trimmings.

French Court Dancer

HEIGHT: 5½ in (140 mm)

The somewhat fanciful attire of this character intentionally appears romantic and artificial for she is employed to dance and entertain at court for the amusement of the aristocracy. She would have worked between 1770 and 1780 at the height of court extravagance before the French Revolution. She is again by doll artist Jill Bennett, who both made and dressed the figure.

Old Regency Lady

Height: 5 ½ in (140mm)

Dressed in what she might consider her finery, this elderly lady is, perhaps, having a little trouble keeping up with the current style. Nevertheless she has real feathers in her bonnet and her sleeves, and her costume has trimmings of antique lace. She is another hand sculpted, portrait painted figure created and dressed by doll artist Marcia Backstrom. She is both signed and numbered, and is one of a kind.

A Regency Lady

HEIGHT: 5 ½ in (140 mm)

By the end of the 18th and the beginning of the 19th centuries, the stiff formality of earlier Georgian fashions was abandoned in favor of simple, elegant designs based on classical Greek styles. Elaborate wigs also became outdated, and a natural hairstyle of hair bound in a chignon and softened by gentle curls became popular. This dainty and beautiful doll, viewed from both back and front with the aid of a carefully positioned mirror, which is also in keeping with the period, epitomizes ladies' fashions between 1800 and 1825. It is the work of Sue Atkinson of the British company Sunday Dolls, which produces patterns and instructions for completing dolls in a number of styles.

Georgian Family Group

HEIGHT: 6 in (153 mm)

This family group of father, mother, and little girl admirably depicts the styles of the 1770s. Here a variety of different types of lace have been used, together with fabrics of cotton and silks, to dress the dolls. As with other figures created by Jill Bennett, they have metal bodies that can be posed, and hand-painted porcelain heads. Note the styling of the gentleman's jacket buttons, collar, and lace cuffs together with the length of his britches and the styling of his wig. Note too the form and length of the mother and daughter's dresses and the open line of the mother's overdress, all typical of the Georgian period.

3

The VICTORIAN ERA

A HOST OF FASCINATING CHARACTERS FROM ALL WALKS OF VICTORIAN LIFE ARE IMMORTALIZED IN MINIATURE.

The Lady with Lorgnettes

HEIGHT: 5 ½–6 in (140-153 mm)

Not everyone dresses in the latest styles at all times. Very often the clothes people wear are actually a few years old. This couple could date anywhere from late Victorian to early Edwardian times. The gentleman's clothing is perhaps more Edwardian in feel, whereas the detail on the lady's skirt shows it to be from a much earlier period. These figures are made and dressed almost entirely of paper and papier-mâché. The gentleman's jacket, waistcoat, and shoes are of kid leather. They are the work of Gale Elena Bantock, who hand-painted each model, and also filled the wood-constructed bureau with an assortment of objets d'art.

Seated Lady

HEIGHT: 5 ½ in (140 mm)

Gale Elena Bantock is the creator of this finely attired lady. However, all is not as it first appears—the entire figure, including face, costume, and hair, has been sculpted exclusively from paper and papier-mâché, and skillfully painted by the artist, helped by her previous occupation as a fine china restorer, to represent the textures and finishes required.

19th-Century Washerwoman

HEIGHT: 5 ½ in (140 mm)

The dress of working people and domestic servants changed little through the middle of the 19th century. This doll by James Carrington stands beside a washtub with a wringer, created by Ian Berry of Miniature Memories, and which would date from 1850. The doll was individually hand-sculpted from polymer clay and has all the character of a hard-working drudge.

"Grave Robbing"

HEIGHT: 6 in (153 mm)

This doll by James Carrington completes a somewhat macabre scene created by Chapel Road Miniatures entitled "Grave Robbing." He is surrounded by the tools of his illegal trade, and appears to have a rat as his companion. His clothes have been soiled and aged with stains and dyes by the doll artist to create an accurate representation of such a disreputable character.

Pearly King and Queen

HEIGHT: 6 in (153 mm)

Here a Pearly King and Queen seem to be enjoying a splendid song and dance. In the East End of London, where they hail from, it would be said that they are having "a right old knees-up," or party. Their clothes are adorned with numerous pearl buttons, following the fashion started in around 1886 among London street vendors. The two would have been elected "king" and "queen" by their fellow traders as leaders or representatives who could be consulted on many matters. The tradition lives on today, although such characters can mostly only be seen at festivals and fêtes. These dolls were made and dressed by artist James Carrington.

Girl in Late Victorian Walking Dress

HEIGHT: 5 ½ in (140 mm)

This doll's outfit is a walking dress, and would date from around 1885. Sue Atkinson designed this outfit, using plain and striped silks, lace edgings, picot braid, ribbons, and leather for the boots to create an entire ensemble. She even made a brooch and earrings from gold chain and gemstones.

The Cratchits

AVERAGE HEIGHT: 5 ½ in (140 mm)

Doll artist James Carrington made these dolls in the form of Bob and Mrs. Cratchit and Tiny Tim from Charles Dickens' *A Christmas Carol*. Each doll is made from polymer clay, and each can be fully posed. They are dressed in natural fabrics in a style that befits the characters—for example, Mrs. Cratchit's apron is dirty and stained.

Two Victorian Ladies

HEIGHT: 5 ½ in (140 mm)

Overheard by a bust of Queen Victoria herself, these two ladies indulge in a little light gossip. Both porcelain dolls were made and dressed by Cookie Ziemba, who molded the hair of one and wigged that of the other. Both dolls have been dressed in costumes made of silk.

Older Women

HEIGHT: 5 ½ in (140 mm)

Marcia Backstrom hand sculpted and oil painted these two polymer clay dolls, dressing them with true Victorian sobriety. They are older ladies who would have dressed almost permanently in black out of respect for the death of one of their friends or aging family. Their arms and legs can be fully posed and they can also bend or sit.

The New World
EARLY AMERICANS

THE DAYS OF THE AMERICAN PIONEERS AND THE WILD WEST ARE BROUGHT TO LIFE IN THIS CAVALCADE OF BEAUTIFULLY MADE CHARACTERS.

Cowboys

HEIGHT: 6 in (153 mm)

These two rugged Western characters would probably date from the latter part of the 19th century. They are the Lawman, who has a Colt .45 in his holster, and One-Eyed Jack, who holds a double-barreled shotgun made from silver and fine wood. Both are the work of International Guild of Miniature Artisans Fellow, Shirley Whitworth, who made the dolls in porcelain from originally designed molds, and their practical, sturdy costumes from natural fabrics. The dolls have body parts that are fully moveable, making them more poseable and, therefore, adding greater realism when they are positioned, standing or sitting down, in a setting.

George and Martha Washington

HEIGHT: 6 in (153 mm)

Factual historical characters do not fit into everyone's miniature settings but Cookie Ziemba embraces them and makes them her own. George Washington, first president of the United States, and his wife, Martha, comfortably "inhabit" Ziemba's Vassal Craigie house, which she has set in approximately 1775.

Hillbilly Lady

HEIGHT: 5 ½ in (140 mm)

Marcia Backstrom's Hillbilly Lady might date from early in the 20th century. Judging by the length of her dress she may be from the 1930s, although her boots seem to be from a slightly earlier time. However, fashion is of little importance to this rustic lady who simply exudes character. Once completed, Backstrom signs and numbers each of her unique one-of-a-kind dolls.

Prudence the Shaker

Height: 5 ½ in (140 mm)

Shirley Whitworth's Prudence probably dates from 1840, when the Shaker movement was at its height. She would have lived in a closed community according to the Shaker's religious beliefs. Her dress and apron are made of cotton, and she carries a basket that would probably have been made by one of the members of her community.

The Boy and the Butterfly

Height: 4 ½ in (114 mm)

Representing little boys everywhere, this little fellow is in a world of his own. He is from the land of Tom Sawyer and Huckleberry Finn, and is the creation of Shirley Whitworth, who works exclusively in porcelain. He is dressed in clothes of cotton which the artist has dirtied in keeping with the character.

Aged Navajo Warrior

HEIGHT: 6 in (153 mm)

Again created by doll artist Shirley Whitworth, this aging Navajo warrior is sadly past his prime. He dreams of earlier days when he was a young man, but refuses to lay down his spear and shield. He would date from the 1860s, and would have inhabited the lands of the American Southwest. His clothes have been made mostly from various fine leathers, and around his neck he wears the silver and turquoise jewelry that was so distinctive of his tribe. He is a porcelain doll with distinctive facial features, and his arms and legs can be fully posed.

Into the TWENTIETH CENTURY

FROM EDWARDIAN SPLENDOR TO WARTIME AUSTERITY—DEPICTED EXPERTLY BY TOP MINIATURISTS.

Forties Femme Fatale

HEIGHT: 5 ½ in (140 mm)

This young lady is evocative of Hollywood style of the 1940s and sits posed to show her dress to best advantage. The dress, on a porcelain doll by artist Sylvia Mobley, is once again the creation of Janet Middlebrook of Miniature Mademoiselle, who designed and made it from fine silk. The fabric flows beautifully and realistically, and note the exquisite pleating on the sleeves and around the hem. The hair, too, has been excellently styled in wonderfully peroxide-blonde fashion, also by Janet Middlebrook. The added silver chair, table, and calla lilies by Sandra Henry Wall in a silver vase complete the perfect 1940s setting.

Having a Party?

HEIGHT: 6 in (153 mm)

The grouping together of two or more dolls can begin to tell a story as the characters start to interact. Even then, like a painting, the scene is open to interpretation, but this is part of the fun for the miniature collector. These figures were all made by doll artist Gudrun Kolenda, who sculpted each face and body from polymer clay. Kolenda certainly intended the figures in striped pants to be butlers, but positioned here with the other two characters one wonders just who is having the party.

Glamour Dolls

HEIGHT: 5 ½ in (140 mm)

Glamorous clothing in the styles of the 1920s and 1930s is just one of the specialties of Janet Middlebrook, who dressed these two porcelain dolls. They represent true Hollywood fashion and are posed in the manner of film stars from the early era of movies. Their costumes have been expertly designed and created from pure silk, with one having cuffs made from real feathers.

Down at the Beach

HEIGHT: 6 ¼ in (159 mm)

Not every dollhouse doll must live indoors, as these two Edwardian bathers prove. They, too, are an excellent example of how a pair of figures can interact and bring a scene to life. If one looks carefully, the young man's toe is raised as though in pain, probably because he has stepped on a crab! In spite of this, he puts on a brave face as the girl looks at him adoringly and admires his muscles. Both are made from porcelain with armatured bodies and can be posed in a number of ways. Her bathing suit is fashioned entirely from silk, while his has been knitted from cotton thread. The two were made by Jill Bennett some years ago.

Old Peasant Lady

HEIGHT: 5 ½ in (140 mm)

The old peasant lady, who holds a tiny baby, dates from the turn of the century. Both she and the baby have been hand-crafted in papier-mâché and hand-painted. They are the work of miniature maker Penny Thompson, who also produces dwellings in which her characters can live.

Lady of 1912

HEIGHT: 5 ½ in (140 mm)

The high waist and "peg top" skirt of this ensemble show the new "emancipated" fashions of 1912, the age of tea dances and tangos. There is a connection here with the figure and theatrical people, who were not then the most respectable. She also smokes a cigarette, another sign of "modern" decadence. These details are all-important to Jill Bennett, who made and dressed this figure.

Flapper Dolls

HEIGHT: 5 ½ in (140 mm)

From the days of the Roaring Twenties come this pair of party-goers, made by Jill Bennett. One is dressed in a blue silk dress with matching feather on a band around her hair, and the other in seemingly sportsman's attire, another fashion of the day. One girl wears the new shorter length skirt, and the other wears a monocle, while both have freshly bobbed haircuts in the latest style.

1940s Family

HEIGHT: 5 ½ in–6 in (140 mm–153 mm)

These proud parents, with baby in its Christening robe, are in typical clothing from the 1940s and would look wonderful in a domestic setting from that date. Note the mother's mid-calf skirt and the father's vest. The dolls are made of porcelain by Michelle Mahler.

FLIGHTS *of* FANCY

DOLLHOUSE MINIATURES DON'T HAVE TO BE DRAWN FROM LIFE. THE ONLY LIMITS ARE THOSE OF THE ARTIST'S IMAGINATION!

An Arabian Knight

HEIGHT: 6 in (153 mm)

This handsome figure was created by Dagmar Jung, who also customized the horse ridden by the figure. Dagmar first crafted the doll from a modern modeling material, and subsequently painted him with acrylic paints in order to achieve the flesh tones she desired. His romantic costume was created from a number of different silks, with his red jacket patterned by designs of fine gold threads. He carries a splendid sword with magnificent silver handle in its sheath. All this, together with the horse's bridle and cover, lend the duo a high degree of realism.

An Old Witch

HEIGHT: 5 ½ in (140 mm)

In the world of fantasy and make-believe fairies, goblins, witches, and demons often dominate. This wonderful old witch, also by Gudrun Kolenda, looks absolutely ancient—she could have inhabited every story ever told. Here she holds her book of spells without which she would be lost. Note her extended fingernails, which remind us of a late 1990s fashion.

Tweedledum and Tweedledee

HEIGHT: 4 in (102 mm)

A polymer clay was the medium used to sculpt these two nursery-rhyme characters by the mother and daughter team who form Little Bloomers. Again, their hands and faces were painted with acrylics after the medium was dry. Their armatured bodies make them fully poseable.

Humpty Dumpty

HEIGHT: 4 in (102 mm)

Humpty Dumpty sat on the wall, or at least here he does! Now made of polymer clay, it is unlikely he would break should he fall, although his arms are completely bendable. Like Tweedledum and Tweedledee, he was made by Little Bloomers and represents part of a series of nursery-rhyme characters made by them.

Santa Claus

HEIGHT: 6 in (153 mm)

Dressed in the costume that preceded the more familiar all-red hat and jacket trimmed with white, this Santa Claus might not be instantly recognizable. The detail of his face and long, untidy hair and beard are superb, and the artist, Gudrun Kolenda, added the details of wire-framed glasses, a cut Christmas tree over the left shoulder, and well-worn leather boots.

Betsy Ross and Uncle Sam

AVERAGE HEIGHT: 6 in (153 mm)

A real person, Betsy Ross has entered American folklore for being the lady who made the first flag for the United States of America featuring the Stars and Stripes. Whether she might have actually appeared as this figure created by Marcia Backstrom is a matter of conjecture, but we certainly would like to think she did. Uncle Sam, on the other hand, was a name used by the United States government, although its origin is sometimes credited to Samuel Wilson, who inspected army supplies in the War of 1812. When the supplies passed inspection and were stamped, they were often referred to as "Uncle Sam." In any event, dressed as he is here in his "Stars and Stripes" he is definitely a fantasy.

Sleeping Beauty

LENGTH: 6 in (153 mm)

Suitable for use in so many different ways, this beautiful porcelain figure asleep in her gilded bed conjures up a whole host of ideas. Janet Middlebrook of Miniature Mademoiselle dressed the doll as well as the bed, and sold the two together. She worked with fine silk and lace trimmings to produce a most enchanting result.

Happy Birthday

HEIGHT: 6 ½ in (153 mm)

By putting together figures from two different makers, a scene has been created that was most probably not in the minds of the original doll artists. Here a mousse cake by Miniature Dreams adds focus to the scene. The figure on the left was made by Gudrun Kolenda of Feathers, Lace, and Clay and has fully poseable arms and legs. The purple dragon on the right is the work of Todd Krueger of Trilogy International. The bodies of each have been made from modern synthetic modeling materials that have been skillfully colored and painted to create the finished effect.

7

THOROUGHLY MODERN MINIATURES

CONTEMPORARY DOLLS FOR CONTEMPORARY SETTINGS: HERE IS A SELECTION OF THE MOST UP-TO-DATE PIECES.

Guys Talking

HEIGHT: 6 in (153 mm)

While many collectors create their dollhouses or miniature settings in some period of the past, a growing number of collectors like to make their scenarios in the present day. These two guys are of the 1990s, and although here it looks like they have just met in the street and are enjoying catching up with the latest news, they could be used almost anywhere. Even when surroundings, furnishings, and accessory items might have styles of an earlier time, there is no reason why they cannot be used in a scene that is set in the present day. These figures were made by doll artist Glenda Hooker who specializes in contemporary, everyday folk, making outfits from modern-day clothing materials.

Diaper Dilemma

HEIGHT: 2 in (51 mm)

No one could resist these tiny tots checking each other out in another little grouping that shows how dolls can interact. Their little characters have been captured perfectly by their creator Gudrun Kolenda, who both made and dressed the figures. Each could again be used in a number of different modern settings. They could be positioned with a toy, or playing with mother, or on top of a diaper changing table.

African Lady

HEIGHT: 5 ½ in (140 mm)

Made by doll artist Glenda Hooker, the character of a smart African lady has been captured beautifully in a figure sculpted from polymer clay. The lady wears a long, cotton dress of dynamic tiger pattern and a lovely necklace of irregularly shaped beads. Here she stands beside a gourd pot made by Andrea Fabrega.

Yuppie Couple

HEIGHT: 6 in (153 mm)

Already a little dated, this Los Angeles couple illustrate how quickly life moves on and how the passing years leave a period in time. Miniatures set in the present day soon become a record of the past, which will hold real fascination in the future. This boy and girl are dressed in the modern fabrics of stretch Lycra and denim, and wear contemporary running shoes.

The Deli Man

HEIGHT: 6 in (153 mm)

The deli man, although very much of today is at the same time almost timeless. His bibbed apron with pockets and his baggy trousers are probably in the same style as he has worn for the last forty years. His dapper bow tie and winged collar obviously date from an earlier time but, worn together with his straw hat, the man still believes he cuts a dash at his downtown delicatessen. In his Shaker-style basket he carries a collection of fresh apples and looks confident that he can sell them. The doll was made and dressed by Gudrun Kolenda and, as with all her figures, simply exudes personality and character.

Index

Credits

I should like to express special gratitude to all those makers who lent their wonderful creations to photograph for this book. Also, thanks to Cookie Ziemba, William Whiting, and Whitledge Associates for permitting me to borrow pieces from their personal collections, and especially to my wonderful wife Esther, whose support never falters.